Remembering Your Story

LEADER'S GUIDE
Revised Edition

Remembering Your Story

Creating Your Own Spiritual Autobiography

LEADER'S GUIDE
Revised Edition

Richard L. Morgan

UPPER ROOM BOOKS®
NASHVILLE

REMEMBERING YOUR STORY
Creating Your Own Spiritual Autobiography
Leader's Guide / Revised Edition
Copyright © 2002 by Richard L. Morgan
All rights reserved.

The Upper Room® Web site http://www.upperroom.org

Scripture quotations not otherwise identified are from the HOLY BIBLE, NEW INTERNATIONAL VERSION. NIV. Copyright 1973, 1978, 1984 by International Bible Society. Used by permission of Zondervan Publishing House. All rights reserved.

Cover Design: Ellisor Design
Interior Design: Gore Studio
Second Printing: 2002

Page 72 serves as an extension of this copyright page.

Library of Congress Cataloging-in-Publication Data
Morgan, Richard Lyon, 1929–
    Remembering your story: leader's guide / by Richard L. Morgan.—
Rev. ed.
        p. cm.
    Includes bibliographical references.
    ISBN 0-8358-0964-1
    1. Middle aged persons—Religious life. 2. Autobiography—Religious aspects—Christianity. 3. Storytelling—Religious aspects—Christianity. 4. Christian aged—Religious life. 5. Autobiography—Authorship. 6. Report writing. I. Title.
Title.

BV4579.5 .M666 2002
248.8'4—dc21   2001045443

Contents

Foreword
Guidance for the Journey

We live in an era when autobiographical and confessional writing is everywhere: on TV, in the tabloids, among self-help groups, and, of course, in psychotherapy of all varieties. In a world drowning in autobiography, why is there any need to offer help in "remembering your story"?

The answer is that our situation today is like *The Rime of the Ancient Mariner*: "Water, water, everywhere, nor any drop to drink." We live in an ocean of autobiographical and confessional writing. But hardly any of it is life-giving, because very little is inspired by a faith-based vision. Therein lies the paradox of our time. Like the Ancient Mariner who will die unless he escapes drinking salt water from the sea, so we too need to find a source of pure water if we are not to die of spiritual thirst.

The need for guidance here is paramount, and that is what *Remembering Your Story* gives us: guidance in spiritual autobiography. Some of the greatest spiritual writers of our time—Thomas Merton and Simone Weil—have raised their prophetic voices to address the basic problem: how to find the "fresh water" of spiritual truth among the stories we tell about ourselves and our lives.

One of the first books of spiritual autobiography, *Confessions* by Saint Augustine, was a work of religious inspiration. "My heart is restless 'till it rests in Thee," was Augustine's poignant prayer to God. He wrote his *Confessions* in a turbulent age, the turn of the fourth century in the Roman Empire. Then, as now after the turn of the century, every option or spiritual lifestyle seemed available. But unlimited choice is not always good. How to choose and make sense of it all? That is our problem too. Always the master exponent of free will, Augustine would not have been surprised by the self-help section of Barnes and Noble. Augustine would have understood immediately. Spiritual guidance faces the challenge of helping people choose among unlimited options.

We face the same problem in telling our life stories: how to choose among all the memories of a lifetime and, finally, how to make sense of our life story. To write a "spiritual" autobiography is to say that, somehow, a horizon beyond our individual lives gives us perspective, helps us make sense of it all. We never quite reach that horizon, but we desperately need help in finding our way across the terrain.

Richard Morgan offers that help in this revised edition of *Remembering Your Story*. In the Leader's Guide he has produced a "map" to help group leaders who will guide others on this journey of autobiographical consciousness.

If this journey were easy, we would not need guidance. But Dr. Morgan points out that whenever an autobiography group comes together, it faces power struggles and a need for commitment —sin and free will again. Group members need to learn to listen, not an easy task. But the group has power that each individual needs, even if every one of us must go on the journey of self-knowledge alone.

Therein lies another paradox: We journey alone yet we need rules; we need a summary of "best practices" in leading autobiography groups. Here Morgan provides such rules and skillful practices. For example, the spiritual lifeline exercise organizes memory into decades of life and imaginatively reconstructs life history in terms of the great Bible stories. This exercise gradually leads participants to realize that each life story is part of a Big Story, just as each of our lives is a link in the chain of generations. Dialogue across generations is itself an old story, an echo of Saint Augustine when he entered into dialogue with his mother and, in the famous vision at Ostia, enjoyed a glimpse of eternity beyond the limits of time.

Much of what leaders do for people in autobiography groups sounds like what takes place in therapy: negotiating life transitions, rediscovering childhood, finding a secret pattern in past experience. Is spiritual autobiography, then, nothing more than an affiliate for the Biography Channel or the mental health network? Not quite. Rational truth, whatever its source, can become part of Christian doctrine. It is not surprising that Plato and Plotinus helped Augustine on his journey to faith.

In the same way, Morgan has surveyed the best, the most profound insights of secular life-span development psychology to find what is true and compatible with religious faith. He has adopted those insights for the purpose of guiding practitioners of spiritual autobiography.

This book abounds in techniques and methods refined by practice. Yet talk of technique or method is perhaps misleading. In the end, this Leader's Guide is an instrument of grace. It is not a final map but rather a mapmaker's guide intended to help each of us on the sacred journey. We must not forget that the map is not the territory and good guidance is never a substitute for going on the journey ourselves. But, with this book, we can hope to make the journey. As T. S. Eliot wrote, "We shall not cease exploring, and the end of all our exploring will be to arrive where we started and know the place for the first time."

HARRY R. MOODY, PH.D.
Director, Institute for Human Values in Aging
Brookdale Center on Aging of Hunter College
Author of *Five Stages of the Soul*

Introduction

Since the seminal work of Robert N. Butler in 1963, doing life review with older persons has become a major task for social workers and clinicians. Life review is no longer seen as meaningless ramblings of older persons but a natural and necessary task of the later years.

The positive effects of life review have been documented by social workers, doctors, nurses, and clergy. It provides a way for older persons to avoid despair, discover the integrity of their lives, and move toward wholeness as persons.

A strategic article by Michael Vitez published in the *Philadelphia Inquirer* (13 February 2000) related how telling one's story had ridden a big wave of popularity as seniors across the nation had created legacies by telling their life stories. He claimed that this growing phenomenon is due to several factors: (1) seniors now live longer and have more time to review their lives; (2) the rapid change in American life and culture makes seniors realize that grandchildren do not understand how grandparents lived or know the major events that shaped their lives; (3) the increased mobility of American society means stories once passed down orally will now be lost unless they are preserved; (4) technology has made preservation a much easier task for older people.

However, only in the past few years has the spiritual dimension of telling stories been added. The faith dimension is often by-passed in the life-review process, with little attention given to where God fits into the life journey. Since its publication in 1996, *Remembering Your Story* has focused on faith stories and added that needed dimension to life review.

Although *Remembering Your Story* began in a nursing home setting to preserve the stories of older persons, the book has had a ripple effect across generations. Many older persons not in nursing homes are highly involved in writing and recording their stories as a legacy for their families. Midlifers, many of whom confront major life transitions, have joined the search for meaning through life stories. For them remembering is a way not only to see patterns of their past but pathways to their future.

The most recent development has been the discovery of the power of our stories to connect generations. Older persons delight when younger people want to hear their stories, and young people, often alienated and cut off from the past, listen with interest to the faith and wisdom of the older generations.

This Leader's Guide exists mainly to guide groups engaged in spiritual autobiography. It also offers helpful suggestions to clergy and clinicians to assist persons of all ages in remembering and preserving their stories. A variety of ways in which *Remembering Your Story* can be used is also presented, as well as strategies for using the book in a group process.

Almost twenty years ago Ann Bedford Ulanov wrote, "Aging brings home to us what we have done or failed to do with our lives, our creativity or our waste, our openness to zealous hiding from what really matters. Precisely at that point, age cracks us open, sometimes for the first time, makes us more aware of the center, makes us look for it and for relation to it."[1]

This Leader's Guide is for all seekers of meaning at any age so we can become more aware of the center of our lives and find meaning for that which remains. If we do not leave behind our faith legacies, how will future generations know them? By snapshots in faded albums? or the contents of a NASA capsule? or our sitcoms? Only we can leave behind the story of the best of what we are and the faith by which we live. This Leader's Guide will help do just that.

WAYS TO USE *REMEMBERING YOUR STORY*

The following ways to use *Remembering Your Story* are based on more than five years of field study in various settings. Any of these strategies can be replicated.

1. *Individual Recording of Stories*
   There is no right or wrong way to record your story.

Some persons prefer to write their story by themselves, working at their computer.

The 100 open-ended questions in the Four Ages Questionnaire (pages 162–66) will guide this process. This is a chronological approach, from childhood to old age.

In her book, *Your Life As Story*, Tristine Rainer calls the imagining of one's life as a continuous line stretching from birth to the present the Submarine Sandwich approach.[2] A person cuts this loaf into slices or chapters, each covering a number of years. Rainer claims some memoirs focus only on a single period of time out of one's life, whether it be childhood or retirement. She calls this *the single slice*. She changes her metaphor from food to needlework and identifies the *embroidery thread* approach to stories, in which a dominant theme becomes the story, and only those times in your life that relate to this theme are preserved.

If you journal your story by yourself, remember there is no right or wrong way. One woman from a small rural town wrote her story like a book, titling each segment of her life by poetic chapters: Spills, Drills, Thrills, Hills, Bills, Ills, Pills, and Wills. Another participant wrote her life story using musical terms such as *rhythm, andante, director, discords, staccato, allegro, rests,* and so on to tell her story.

Another woman in one of my workshops told her story through quilting. She brought quilts to the group which she had made representing various persons and events in her life story. The quilts became a narrative, as she used needlework and cloth to capture her life's joys and sorrows.

2. *Sharing Stories with Another Person*

Experience has shown that some persons remember their stories best in dialogue with another person. At times that person may be a spiritual friend who takes time to listen. Everyone longs to tell his or her story to someone and have it accepted and understood.

At other times, it can be a friend who videotapes your

story. Home video techniques can help older persons tell their stories. Questions on pages 167–68 of *Remembering Your Story* provide memory joggers.

Some older people now share some of their stories with children and grandchildren through E-mail. In a recent group in New York City, a woman shared with us that she was sending E-mails to all her grandchildren, telling them the story of how she and her family hid from the Nazis during the occupation of Holland.

One of the most powerful ways to preserve stories of older persons who need help in this task is through interviews by young people. Several projects have already taken place using this model. Young people were recruited, trained to do interviewing, and then commissioned to spend time with an elder of their own choice. They used questions on pages 167–68 of *Remembering Your Story* as the basis of their interview, which they did by videotape. On the back porches of shut-in members, by the bedsides or wheelchairs of members in nursing homes, they patiently listened and taped their stories. At a special church night dinner called "Across the Generations," old and young sat together as each young person shared a faith story learned from an older friend.

In each of these scenarios, the one who records the story must be a good listener and willing to be focused on the other person's story. Neil Wyrick has shown the need for such listeners in his poem, "On the First Shelf of the Library of Heaven":

> *I talked to the Lord, but did not listen.*
> *I demanded to be heard, but assigned no such*
> *   importance to the views of others.*
> *And so it was that one day when I entered at the*
> *   gates of heaven*
> *A large book with my name on it lay open.*
> *And reading its title page I wept,*

For printed in gold were the words
Listen unto others as you would have them
 listen unto you.
And too many pages were blank.[3]

3. *Settings for the Group Process*
    Experience has proved that sharing and writing sto-
ries in a group setting is the best way to help persons
remember their stories. *Remembering Your Story* has been
written for a ten-week group study but can be adapted to
other settings as well. *Remembering Your Story* has been
used in a variety of ways and in many different settings.

- Church school hour class (older adults or intergener-
  ational)
- Wednesday evening class (older adults or intergener-
  ational)
- Training hospice staff and volunteers
- Midlifers in times of transition
- Retirement communities (for residents and/or staff)

    Remembering Your Story has also been used in a
retreat setting, for new-member assimilation, training
church officers, or spending a weekend in sharing stories
across generations. See Appendix 2 (pages 70–71) for
explicit instructions to lead a weekend retreat.

LEADING A GROUP PROCESS

Preparing to Remember

Forming a Group

An effective group may consist of as few as five or six adults who
come together to share life stories. The best group size is ten to
twelve adults. With more than twelve people, form smaller groups.
Some adult church school classes have chosen to study *Remembering Your Story* as a group at an alternate time during the week;
other churches have begun new small groups.

Participants need a copy of *Remembering Your Story* at least a week before the group meets for the first time. Order books from Customer Service, Upper Room Books, 1908 Grand Avenue, Nashville, TN 37212 or call toll-free 1-800-972-0433. Plan ahead and allow three weeks for delivery.

An Invitation

The following may serve as an invitation to the group experience:

You are invited to join a *Remembering Your Story* group that will meet at _____
on _____ from _____ to _____.
The group will meet weekly for 90 minutes per session.

You will view the events of your own life and listen appreciatively to other people's stories, as we share and write our stories. Working both in a small group and with a spiritual friend you will recall your own faith story, listen to others' faith stories, reflect on biblical stories, and preserve your story as a legacy.

All participants will write both during class and between sessions and will be encouraged to share their work with another group member or the group. (Sharing is encouraged but voluntary.) Writing experience is not necessary.

The group will use the book *Remembering Your Story*, written by Richard L. Morgan. Group leadership will be provided by _____. For further information contact _____.

Group Process

Every group meeting offers the possibility of forming community. When stories are shared, the moment is present for intimacy and ultimacy to occur in groups. My brother, Dr. John C. Morgan, has identified five stages in the formation of spiritual communities.[4]

"The first stage of a spiritual community is that of excitement, new energy, 'the honeymoon.'" Although the group is still fragile, there is a sense of excitement and expectancy in the first moments.

"The second stage is the beginning of a power struggle, with

some folks demanding control and acting out their need for it."
Grandstanders may monopolize the group, and even when
another group member speaks, they may fail to notice and persist
in dominating the group. The risk here is that this need to control
can deenergize the group.

*"If the community survives those who storm out, it reaches a
third stage of stability.* People learn to take responsibility for their
actions and listen to others. A sense of community begins to
develop because of shared experience.

The fourth stage is that of commitment. The group members
begin to experience the sense of "we" and not just "me" and
become more interdependent.

*The fifth stage of cooperation occurs when group members cre-
ate their own community and stories.*

Group Leadership

This Leader's Guide will offer instructions for each of the ten sessions. However, do not feel that you have to "get through" all the
suggested activities. Choose those that seem most pertinent to
your particular group. *What is of primary importance is the group
process and the sharing of stories between partners.* As a leader you
will model the suggested activities for the rest of the group. Your
presence is extremely important, since the material may evoke
strong emotions within the group.

One person may lead all the sessions, or two people may co-
lead, alternating sessions. In church settings, pastors, associate
pastors, or Christian educators often lead groups. Church school
teachers, youth workers, or other church leaders may provide leadership in a faith community setting. If groups meet in retirement
communities or health care centers, social workers, chaplains, or
activities directors could provide leadership.

Be sure the group meets in a well-lighted, airy room with space
for both group sessions and one-on-one interaction. Arrange the
room by placing chairs in a circle. As you select a location, by all
means consider the needs of persons with handicapping conditions.

Leading a *Remembering Your Story* group can be a rich, spiritual experience. Your presence will enable those gathered to share their faith journeys and find wholeness in their lives.

May this prayer of Thomas à Kempis be in your heart as you lead others:

> *Grant, O Lord, to all students, to love*
> *that which is worth loving, to know*
> *that which is worth knowing, to praise*
> *that which pleaseth thee most, to*
> *esteem that which is most precious*
> *unto thee, and to dislike whatsoever is*
> *evil in thine eyes. Grant that with true*
> *judgment they may distinguish things*
> *that differ, and, above all, may search*
> *out and do what is well-pleasing unto*
> *thee; through Jesus Christ our Lord.*
> *Amen.*

1

From Memory to Faith: Life Stories

OVERVIEW

The aim of this study is to help participants realize the importance of sharing and preserving their stories as legacies for future generations. The level of sharing is a personal decision, as one's privacy is always protected, but sharing is expected of each member. Trust is essential and will develop as the group members bond together.

PREPARATION

Copies of *Remembering Your Story* should be given to group members before the first session. Participants are asked to read chapter 1. Have available for each participant a four-by-six-inch index card, pencil or pen, and a copy of the "Underlying Philosophy of the Group" (found on the next page). You may prefer to print the "Underlying Philosophy of the Group" on newsprint so all may see it.

LEADING THE SESSION

As a warm-up exercise invite participants to find a person they do not know and sit beside her or him. Hand each participant a four-by-six-inch card and a pencil and give these directions:

1. Write your name in large letters in the center of the card.
2. In the upper left-hand corner of the card, write the year you were born and the leader of your country that year.
3. In the upper right-hand corner of the card, write a significant geographical place in your life story.

4. In the lower left-hand corner of the card, write the name of a person who has influenced your life.
5. In the lower right-hand corner of the card, write a place or time where God was present in your life.

Allow the group to complete the task. Then ask each partner to relate this information to the other. Remind the partners they will have no more than ten minutes for both to share their answers. When the group reconvenes, they are to introduce their friend to the group.

After the initial exercise, hand out the following *Underlying Philosophy of the Group* and ask for any discussion.

Underlying Philosophy of the Group

- We need to take time to hear one another, especially our stories. This process of talking and listening gives people the chance to tell their stories.
- Participation is voluntary; confidentiality is encouraged. To tell our story and listen to other stories in a supportive environment demands that we learn to trust one another.
- Those who would become "creative listeners" for others must first share their own stories.
- Groups begin with the Spiritual Lifeline exercise, which becomes the foundation for sharing faith journeys.
- Participants are urged to record their stories as part of the group experience. This process continues even when the group meetings cease.
- This is a spiritual growth group, not a discussion class or a therapy group.

Direct participants' attention to the commitments listed on newsprint or read the covenant aloud to the group. If you made a copy for each participant, pass out the copies now. Affirm that group members need to make preliminary commitments in the form of the following covenant:

I commit myself to

❶ meet with our group during its sessions, only missing because of emergencies.

❷ listen to others and keep group sharing confidential.

❸ participate in the group exercises, with the understanding that what is shared is entirely a matter of personal decision.

❹ spend some private time in meditation, prayer, or other spiritual practice to reflect on the group experience.

❺ check in with the group before I make a decision to leave it.

After reviewing the philosophy and ground rules carefully, ask group members to turn to the Life Map exercise on page 34 of their participant's books. Take a few minutes to explain this exercise. Ask that they take some time this week to develop a personal life map of their story. They are to bring their maps to the next session.

Remind participants that every person is a unique life story that needs to be shared and preserved. Reinforce the fact that younger generations are out of touch with their family stories, which are the legacies we leave. *As we have received them from our ancestors, so we must leave them for future generations.* Direct group members' attention to the diagram on page 20 and make them aware of the interconnectedness of our stories and God's story.

Raise these questions:

- In what ways do you believe that every story is unique?
- What is your response to persons who feel that the "rambling on" of older persons is boring? What has been your experience with older adults and their telling of stories?
- Some persons shy away from remembering their stories for fear of dredging up painful memories. In what ways might the recollection of painful memories be a positive experience?
- Suppose you never told anyone—even family members—about your life story. Would that make a difference to you? to them?

More reasons to record stories

A former group outlined the following reasons why we need to record our stories: (1) no one else will do it for you; (2) no one else knows the stories of your life like you do; (3) your faith story will let your descendants know that you were a real person; (4) the stories you heard from your grandparents will not die out with you; (5) you can work through some of your painful memories and feel at peace having written them down. Ask the group for their reasons for sharing their stories in the group.

LOOKING AHEAD

Tell the participants that they will be reading *Remembering Your Story* as a guide to reflection on their own life stories and as a basis for involvement in the life of the group. The assignment for next week is chapter 2, "The Spiritual Lifeline." Ask that they complete the Seasons of One's Life exercise (pages 32–33) and only *read* about the spiritual lifeline. Explain that they will have time to work on the lifeline exercise during next week's session. For those who enjoy the writing aspect, relay the writing assignment for chapter 2 (see Appendix 1, page 68).

CLOSING

Ask group members to stand in a circle, holding hands as you read Edith Sinclair Downing's words, "As We Look Back in Memory" (page 24). Then ask the group to read in unison Richard Morgan's poem "An Untold Story: Group Process as a Pilgrimage" (pages 26–27). Close in silence.

2

The Spiritual Lifeline

OVERVIEW

It is important to get a broad, telescopic view of one's life story at the outset, before focusing on particular events in one's life. The spiritual lifeline is a critical foundation exercise for remembering one's story. An alternate exercise involves looking at places where one has lived and identifying key events that occurred at these places.

PREPARATION

Group members should have read chapter 2 of the participant's book and completed the Seasons of One's Life exercise before the session. Have red pens or pencils available for participants. If you choose to use the alternate exercise, print the grid of the decades on newsprint or make copies for group members.

LEADING THE SESSION

Ask the group what month (ages) the participants represent. Invite group members to say aloud some of the significant moments in their calendars of life (for example: April, marriage; May, first child; September, retirement; and so on).

Repeat the exercise by asking the group members to say aloud the best time in their life by the month on the calendar.

The Spiritual Lifeline Exercise

The total group begins the work on the spiritual lifeline. Pass out pencils and the red pens or pencils. The following guidelines are important:

❶ Conduct this exercise in a reflective manner with no group comments except questions for clarification.

❷ Be clear about how participants compute their PD (projected death date).

❸ Consider modeling the spiritual lifeline by drawing your own.

❹ Allow group members randomly to call out *historic* events that have taken place during their lifetime. Record these events on newsprint.

❺ Lead the group (step 2) to jot down *celebrations* above the lifeline in the ovals (see page 36) and the *crises* below the lifeline in the ovals. Stress that the celebrations and crises encompass the past, the present, and the future. Remind participants to write just a word or phrase.

    The ovals above the line are remembered as positive and celebrative events of one's life. Beneath the lifeline, significant crises or difficulties are given titles. Each circle is then tied like a balloon to the lifeline at its approximate time of occurrence. Once the lifeline is constructed, further possibilities for adding to it will emerge in the group process.

❻ Jot down in red pencil or pen how group members now perceive God's presence in these moments.

Alternate Exercise

Read the following poem and ask participants to jot down celebrations and crises.

Two Boxes

I have in my hands two boxes, which God gave me to hold.
God said, "Put all your sorrows in the black
and all your joys in the gold."
I heeded his words, and in the two boxes
both my joys and sorrows, I stored.
But though the gold became heavier each day,
the black was light as before.
With curiosity, I opened the black box;

I wanted to find out why.
And I saw in the base of the box,
a hole which my sorrows had fallen out by.
I showed the hole to God and mused aloud,
"I wonder where my sorrows could be?"
He smiled a gentle smile at me and said,
"My child, they're all here with me."
I asked, "God, why give me the boxes,
why the gold and the black with the hole?"
"My child," God said, "the gold is for you
to count your blessings,
the black is for you to let go."

A Word about Dyads or Pairing

Dyads help people reflect and share, allowing every group member to tell his or her story. In setting up dyads ask participants to choose a partner whom they do not know well. The overall dyad should last twenty minutes, and should be structured so that during the first ten minutes one person shares his or her story, with the second person listening quietly, only intervening to ask questions. In the second ten-minute period, the second person speaks, and the first person listens.

After the dyads have formed, ask each person to tell his or her partner some event or insight from the spiritual lifeline exercise. You may need to remind participants to take time to listen to their partner.

After twenty minutes call the group back together in a circle. Allow a volunteer to share his or her experience. You may ask for general feelings about the sharing time, or pose such a question such as this:

Did you find that you talked more about celebrations or crises in your life story?

Alternate Exercise (as time permits)

The Decades of Your Life

If you choose to pursue this exercise with the group, please print the following grid on newsprint for participants to copy during the session or make copies of this grid for their use.

1920–1930	1930–1940	1940–1950	1950–1960	1960–1970	1970–1980	1980–1990	1990–2000	2000–2010

Say to participants: "Please place your pen in the middle of the decade in which you were born, and begin drawing a line that indicates where your life was during that decade. As I read off the decades, you will have one minute for each decade to chart a line with upturns or downturns showing your life at that time or what you have experienced in that decade of life.

"When you have finished drawing your life up to the present time, reflect on the following questions:

1. What were the best decades of your life thus far? Why?
2. What were the worst decades of your life thus far? Why?
3. What role did your spiritual life play in the process?
4. Where are you now in your life journey?

"You will pair off with a partner and discuss your responses."

LOOKING AHEAD

Next week's reading is chapter 3, "The River of Life." Suggest that participants look up the scriptures mentioned in the chapter as they reflect on the significance of rivers in the biblical story. Tell them that the group will focus on the River of Life guided meditation (page 46), which they may do alone in a quiet place and then reflect on their experience in one of the following ways: by drawing of the river, by making notes on their experience with the exercise, or even writing some poetry. They may represent their river in any way they choose. For those who enjoy the writing aspect, relay the writing assignment for chapter 3 (see Appendix 1, page 68).

CLOSING

Close by reading the "Prayer of Thanksgiving for the Seasons of Life" (page 39) aloud responsively with group members reading the refrain in bold italics.

3
The River of Life

OVERVIEW

One powerful way to be in touch with one's life story is through visualization of the past. Visualization is a meditation-like experience in which persons can recall specific images through a fantasy exercise. In this session the image of a river evokes memories of a person's life from beginning to the present.

PREPARATION

Participants should bring their personal reflections from The River of Life exercise. It will be interesting to compare these experiences with their reflections from the same exercise in a group setting. Have newsprint, markers, and Bibles for each small group.

LEADING THE SESSION

Form four small groups. Pass out Bibles and ask each group to read one of the following scripture passages, focusing on the river in the story.

- Genesis 32:22-32
- Psalm 46
- Psalm 137
- Matthew 3:13-17

Group Process

Step 1   Each group reads and meditates on the Bible passage, recording on newsprint the river's significance.

Step 2 Reconvene the total group and ask each to report on its findings.

Step 3 Summarize the significance of rivers in the Bible story. Record on newsprint if desired.

The River of Life Guided Meditation

The participants have experienced this meditation in a personal way. Now invite them to relax as you lead them through the same meditation in this group setting (page 46).

At meditation's end, give the group time to process the experience. Some may choose to make notes; others may prefer to sit in silence. Allow some time for personal reflection, and then encourage all group members to speak. Suggest that they listen attentively to one another, giving no interpretation or analysis.

Alternate Exercise

Visualize This Scene

Tell the group that thousands of years ago, clans gathered around campfires to hear stories of their past, stories of epic battles, great floods, and meaningful births. As the children listened they learned who they were and what kind of people they were expected to be. Then ask the group to participate in this exercise:

Imagine you lived in the time of King Solomon, and your grandparents began telling you about the crossing of the Jordan River (Joshua 4:1-7).

What would they tell you about the meaning of the twelve stones placed in the middle of the Jordan River?

Imagine you lived in the time of Ezra the scribe, and at a campfire stories were told of your ancestors when they sat by the rivers of Babylon, captives in a strange land (Psalm 137).

What would you hear about the feelings of your ancestors as they sat by those rivers and thought of their home in Judah?

Alternate Exercise

The River of Life

Imagine you are sitting by the banks of a river. Perhaps you can visualize a river that you recall from childhood. As you watch the river flow, you sense that this is the river of your life, flowing like time before you.

You imagine that the material things, your cherished possessions are cast into the river; you watch the current sweep them away; they disappear from view.

You imagine that all your accomplishments and achievements are also cast into the river; you watch them floating away, disappearing from sight.

You realize these things you had and those things you did are not the river. You realize that you are the river, and you go beyond what you have had or done. How does that make you feel?

After the group has responded to the exercise, read the following poem by eighty-year-old Carter Ossman Muller, "The Delta," and ask the group to share how Muller likens her life story to a river.

> As water trickles thru earth and rock
> A spring is born to catch the overflow.
> Somewhere a tiny sperm fights for his own egg cell
> A baby child unfolds.
>
> Over the pebbles a brook
> Runs and gurgles as the river grows.
> Children gurgle—laugh—cry and learn
> They too must grow.
>
> Our life like the river—courses
> Downstream, round and about
> Gathering strength. Pell-mell over
> Precipices, meandering across the plains.
>
> Onward and onward, thru city and farm
> Sometimes peaceful, often carrying loads

The river seeks home in the ocean.
We seek the home of our Spirit Souls.

The Delta is our last resting place
Before we join the mist of the mysteries
To enter our Source,
To meet our God, our Creator.

We hesitate and may tarry.
Our burdens rich and poor
Are dropped—new channels
Are cut. The old is left behind.

As we cross the last edge of life
The mist will burn off.
A new life will say, "Welcome" and
My spirit-soul will be looking for my dear ones,
Whom I expect to see.

Christ promised life after death
Jesus died to convince us
That where He went
We would follow.

Water from the river
Enters the ocean
To rise again
Through clouds, back into
The ground and rocks of earth.

Man [humanity] attached to the Great Spirit
Will go on
Wherever led
Into the Universe.
Our Father, Jesus and the Holy Spirit
Enfolding our awareness.

LOOKING AHEAD

The reading assignment for the next session is chapter 4, "Reclaiming Childhood Stories." Tell participants to draw the floor plan of their childhood home (page 56). Encourage them to recall some of their favorite secret places from their childhood, as well as to consider their childhood conceptions of God.

CLOSING

Ask the members to join hands and form a circle as a group member reads aloud the "Prayer of Thanksgiving" (page 50).

4

Reclaiming Childhood Stories

OVERVIEW

Childhood is a crucial time in anyone's life story. The rules, scripts, and beliefs we learned in childhood persist into later life. This session will help participants relive childhood memories and discern how those experiences have colored their life story.

PREPARATION

Say, "You may recall from The River of Life exercise that you thought about how your life began and what were the tributaries or influence of your childhood. During this session you will take a closer look at your childhood." This session requires paper and a pencil or pen for each participant.

LEADING THE SESSION

One way to trigger memories is to respond to concise questions about one's past. For the next several group sessions, an excellent warm-up is to take ten minutes for triggering memories.

Follow this procedure:

- Arrange participants in two rows facing each other.
- Ask a series of questions, giving thirty seconds for one person to respond and thirty more seconds for the other across from him or her to respond.
- Follow the same process with memory joggers as time permits.

Do *not* allow discussion at this time.

Memory Joggers

- What was your favorite childhood pet; what was its name?
- Recall your favorite radio or television program as a child.
- What song did you enjoy as a child?
- What was a favorite Bible story from childhood?

Four Ages of Life

You might ask group members to take turns reading aloud the brief descriptions of the four ages of life (pages 54–55). Ask them how these descriptions ring true in their experience and about what feels inaccurate.

Floor Plan of a Childhood Home

Pursue this exercise individually with no group response. Ask members if they have finished drawing the floor plans of their childhood homes. For those who have not finished this task, invite them to turn to page 56 in the participant's book and read the information under "Childhood Memories." Then allow time for them to draw their floor plans, either in the participant book or on a separate sheet of paper. Other options may include drawing a diagram or a picture of the house, or they may choose simply to jot down memories in words.

Persons who have completed the task may move on to considering their next choice. Ask them to choose one room in the house that has the happiest memories and best associations, trying to remember every item that was in that room. Some of the following questions may stimulate their thinking and memories:

- What furniture was in the room?
- What pictures, plaques, or bric-a-brac were on the walls?
- What were your favorite TV or radio programs at that time? favorite books?

If a participant cannot think of a room with happy memories, suggest a backyard, a hiding place, or another place from childhood.

Alternate Exercise

Roberta Bondi, in her book *Houses: A Family Memoir of Grace,* suggests that a house is a metaphor for the inner life. She tells some of her life story by recalling the homes where she lived. She meets her true self by rifling through poignant childhood memories, and we meet vivid family characters whose lives were intertwined with hers in those houses.

Ask the group members to recall all the houses where they lived as children, and the people who lived with them in those houses. Ask them to jot down memories that return from those houses.

Suggest that partners talk in pairs about their floor plans, diagrams, or word memories. Each person may then tell about "special rooms," if comfortable doing so. An excellent source for this exercise is Frederick Buechner's book *The Longing for Home* (HarperSanFrancisco, 1996), in which he graphically describes his grandmother's home.

Reconvene the group and read aloud Roberta C. Bondi's words about outgrowing her childish view of God (page 61), or look at the list of inadequate conceptions of God (page 62). Invite group members to share their childhood experiences or conceptions of God.

LOOKING AHEAD

The reading assignment for the next session is chapter 5, "Family Relationships, Family Stories." Ask the group members to try the clustering exercise under "Family Relationships" (pages 66–67) or to identify the roles of their family members (pages 69–70). Suggest that they find photographs from their past—either those that picture them alone or with family or friends—and caption the photos with dates or brief descriptions. If possible, they should bring photos to the next group gathering. See Denis Ledoux, *The Photo Scribe: A Writing Guide/How to Write the Stories behind Your Photographs* (Soleil Press, 1999) for additional help. For those who enjoy the writing aspect, relay the writing assignment for chapter 5 (see Appendix 1, page 69).

CLOSING

Close by forming a circle and reading the prayer litany (pages 62–63), perhaps having one person read the main body of the text and the group's responding with the petition in bold italics. Then read this prayer to the group:

> *Loving Parent, we treasure our child-hood memories, both happy and sad. We know who we are now goes back to those days long ago. Transform the present into moments of magic, as we recall our Christmases as children, happy birthday parties, and family trips. When we remember sad times, help us to see even those times in a new light, always remembering how Jesus said, "Unless you...become like little children, you will never enter the kingdom of heaven" (Matt. 18:2, NIV). Amen.*

5

Family Relationships, Family Stories

OVERVIEW

The family is the crucible in which our stories begin and which continues to affect the rest of our lives. It is true that family stories have the power to shape our lives. This chapter leads participants to look at family relationships and roles and at early sibling relationships. It also identifies control dramas that begin in childhood and continue throughout life.

PREPARATION

Group members have studied roles and relationships from their family of origin and brought photographs that tell the stories of their family life. Provide copies of the questions for "Memories around the Family Table," or write the questions on newsprint.

LEADING THE SESSION
Memory Joggers with a Partner

- Tell about a memory of a happy family vacation.
- Recall a family story often retold.
- Tell about a memory from your church life as a family.
- Tell about occasions that brought your family together.

Choose one of these exercises to get the group involved in looking at family roles and relationships.

Express the hope that members brought at least one photograph to the session. Explain, "Photographs are mirrors with memories. They reflect ourselves back to us across time. They also show how we and our relationships have changed over the years. You have brought with you some photographs of your life. With a partner, interview each other about these photos using such questions as these: Who is in the photo? What does the photo say about you? about other people in the picture?

Family Sculpting

One powerful way to work through family relationships and family stories is through family sculpting. At times it serves as a more effective way to deal with family issues than talking about them. Probably you will need to model this experience for the group unless another member seems willing to try it. Use the following steps as group members watch in silence.

- Choose participants to represent members of your family of origin.
- Direct the drama yourself; choose another person to represent you in the sculpture.
- Give each person his or her cues on how to act within the family scenario. During the sculpting, everyone is to remain silent.
- Place the family members in positions, suggesting facial expressions and body language to represent family roles or relationships (such as Father in a dominant place; Mother submissive, hiding behind Father; one Brother standing apart from the rest of the family; a Brother and Sister in each other's faces).
- Direct family members to "freeze" in position for a few minutes, after which the group members discuss what they saw and felt about the situation.

Ordinarily session constraints allow time to "sculpt" only one family, but you may choose to use the exercise at another time or in another session.

Or

38

Ask the group to pair up, and then hand out the following questions for dialogue:

Memories around the Family Table (Family of Origin)

1. Where did the members sit around the family table? (You might even ask participants to draw the usual seating arrangement.)
2. Where did you sit? Any reason?
3. Was talking encouraged? Who dominated the conversation?
4. When your father was absent from the table, who sat in his place?
5. Who set the agenda for the table talk?
6. Who did the cooking in your house?
7. What quarrels or conflicts can you recall at the table?
8. How did mealtimes change as you grew older?

Allow time for the group to discuss Redfield's control dramas (page 71), especially how those roles were played out in their family of origin.

Alternate Exercise

Create a sociodrama around a family table at dinner time. Role-play the following characters: grandfather, grandmother, mother, father, and five children in the family playing the following roles:

Star: younger sister, outstanding student, destined to attend a major college; her family's pride and joy.

Nurturer: older sister, twenty-five years old; unmarried and stays home to care for grandparents.

Scapegoat: younger sister in her late teens, always the one blamed for everyone else's mistakes; becomes the one everyone picks on.

Clown: high school-aged brother, the constant joker.

Lost child: younger brother, apparently unwanted.

Choose a topic for dinner table discussion; each person plays his or her role. The sociodrama may continue as long as it stays on task and the roles are clear. The leader will call an end to the sociodrama and then invite the group members to discuss the various roles and their own observations.

LOOKING AHEAD

Chapter 6 points to how stories connect generations. Ask the group to do the following:
1. If any of their grandparents are living, they should try to call or visit them before the next group.
2. If all are deceased, they should look for photos of the grandparents and ask parents to tell some of their stories.
3. Finally, ask participants to find out (using a family Bible or history) the following data about parents and grandparents: birth, death, marriage.

For those who enjoy the writing aspect, relay the writing assignment for chapter 6 (see Appendix 1, page 69).

CLOSING

Suggest that group members visualize their families of origin. Urge them to be patient with others because they also have shortcomings. Ask the group, "If you can't make yourself what you want to be, how can you expect to remake somebody else?"

We seek perfection in others yet ignore our own faults. But God has seen to it that we carry each other's burdens (Gal. 6:2):

For no one is without fault,
no one is without burden,
no one is self-sufficient,
no one is wise enough on his [or her] own.
Therefore, we must support one another, comfort one
    another, help, teach, and caution one another.

Close by reading "A Litany for the Generations" (page 75), group members responding with the words in bold italics.

40

6

Stories Connect Generations

OVERVIEW

Family history is crucial to understanding our own history. Our mobile society has isolated generations. The five generational types are described, and three generations are identified in one's family. Family faith stories serve to remind us of the values that have been handed down to our generation.

PREPARATION

Members of the group have identified pertinent data of parents and grandparents (such as birth, death, marriage). Photos and other mementos have also been collected. Each participant needs an index card and a pen or pencil. Make copies of the dialogue "Across the Generations" if each reader is to have his or her own material. The two readers may simply share the Leader's Guide for this exercise. Bring a walking stick or cane to symbolize the talking stick that group members may hold while participating in the Circle of Wisdom.

LEADING THE SESSION

Circle of Generations

If all generations are not represented in the group, ask for volunteers to role-play the generations; it is essential that all five generations be represented in the circle.

Give each participant an index card and ask the group to form a circle of generations, from the youngest (Millennials) to the oldest (Civics). Leave blank spaces in the circle for generations yet to be born and for generations that have died. Ask members of the circle to write their generation in the upper left-hand corner and one word that describes their generation in the upper right-hand corner. After the cards have been filled in, ask members of each generation to share their words aloud.

You may choose any one of the following exercises for connecting generations:

1. Briefly describe the five generations. Ask the group for a representative from each of the five generations. Let the group choose an issue for discussion, such as discipline in the family, the role of women in society, drugs, violence, etc. Ask each generation to speak briefly to that issue, and let the group interact with them and with each other.

2. Match up two generations, having the younger generation interview the older generation to discover the things they share in common and the things they find different about one another's lives. Ask the group to record reactions to the dialogue and then discuss the differences and commonalities among generations.

3. Choose two members of the group to read "Across the Generations: A Dialogue" by Donovan Drake and Dick Morgan. (Either copy the dialogue, or let the two participants share the Leader Guide.) Encourage the group to discuss this dialogue.

Circle of Wisdom

Elder councils played a major role in Native American nations. Sitting in a circle, all were free to speak their mind. Participants formed a circle, symbolic of equality, harmony, and wholeness. In the middle stood a "talking stick," which gave a member of the circle the permission to speak.

Form a wisdom circle with group members role-playing different generations. Any type of stick or cane can be the "talking stick." Give the following instructions:

1. When you want to speak, go to the center, and return to your seat with the "talking stick," which permits you to speak.
2. Begin your sharing on the subject with the word "and...."
3. Add to what others have said without judging their words.
4. Close your sharing with the words, "I have spoken," returning the "talking stick" to the center of the room.
5. After a period of silent reflection, another member of the circle may reach for the talking stick.

In a larger group the "talking stick" can pass clockwise around the circle. Choose any one of the following subjects, and let the wisdom circle take place.

- *As a younger person, what would you want to learn from an older person?*
- *As an older person, what would you like to learn from a younger person?*
- *Describe one lesson life has taught you thus far.*
- *If you knew you had only a few months to live, what would you want to do?*

Across the Generations: A Dialogue

by Donovan Drake and Dick Morgan

NOTE: *The following dialogue by Donovan Drake (age: in his forties) and Dick Morgan (age: in his seventies) attempts to present some of the views of the boomer and adaptive generations. But they do not necessarily reflect the views of the writers:*

Ager: Believe it or not, I am not really one of those greedy geezers interested only in my entitlements, but I really am concerned for what happens when your generation becomes older.

Boomer: I am concerned whether Social Security will be there or not. I am led to believe that it will either collapse or

	resort to becoming a minor subsidy for retirees. And what will happen to the economy if we withdraw our mutual funds all at the same time? These are concerns your generation has never faced.
Ager:	True, but not all of us are affluent or financially secure, because many of us did not prepare for our retirement.
Boomer:	Well, we are alike on that one. I am concerned that my generation and the Gen Xers continue to buy cars on lease, spend on credit, and ignore the need to save for "retirement."
Ager:	Do you feel any resentment that your generation supports our Social Security, whereas thirty years from now you won't have that luxury? Fewer workers to support a greater number of older people.
Boomer:	I don't envy any of your generation getting all the help you can. You've earned it. But I do feel some anger that the wealthy in your midst take their entitlements and their Medicare, even when they have the best financial security possible.
Ager:	I understand. By the year 2020, 210 billion dollars will be spent on Medicare, whereas only 105 billion dollars is spent now. How can the government afford that?
Boomer:	Furthermore, I'm resigned to working past seventy, and perhaps until I die. I don't mind staying active, but I hate to think I cannot know the freedom from the pressure of work like your generation does. It just doesn't seem fair.
Ager:	I know. But the day has gone when "retirement" means sitting in a rocking chair and doing nothing. But we do have the luxury of finding the creative balance between some work and needed rest. Medical technology has extended our life span, and none of us really wants to rust out. But health care for us is a real issue. God knows what it will be for you!

Boomer: Health care. There's the rub! I have to deal now with what to do for my aging parents…you know, assisted living or nursing home. God knows what it will be like for us. Will we end up with disco music in a nursing home? It is sad that the family system has broken down in our society. Everyone looks out for themselves, and it is sad how families have collapsed.

Ager: You mean that in former generations you found adult children keeping their aged parents at home, and that has gone….But we are making plans for those years now, trying to be proactive about it, and not becoming a burden to our children.

Boomer: Good, but many of your generation don't do that planning and we become stretched between our children's needs and our parents' needs. And the way medical science has prolonged life (some say our generation may well live beyond 100), the issues that presents are awesome.

Ager: The more we talk the more I realize we have much in common and need to work together on these issues. What is the best gift our generation can give yours?

Boomer: Give us a positive model of creative aging that focuses on genuine involvement in life and graceful living. We need your stories, your wisdom. Growing old for us will be better if you can do that!

Further Information on Ethical Wills

Barry K. Baines has compiled *The Ethical Will Resource Kit,* available from Brochins Book and Gift Shop (1-877-827-7323). Further information is available at info@ethicalwill.com. In the Resource Kit you will find more background information on ethical wills and examples of how to write an ethical will. It also helps a person create the first draft of an ethical will and provides space for note-taking and jotting down ideas. Group members may wish to develop their ethical wills as a love letter to their family.

LOOKING AHEAD

Next session's reading assignment is chapter 7, "Facing Life's Transitions." Tell group members to read and reflect on the questions under Taking Stock at Midlife and Taking Stock at Retirement (pages 94–95). They may wish to revisit their spiritual lifeline in chapter 2, identifying and highlighting transitions in their stories. For those who enjoy the writing aspect, relay the writing assignment for chapter 7 (see Appendix 1, page 69).

CLOSING

Form the circle of generations again and ask a group member to read "The Last Spring of My Grandmother," by Nancy Yost (page 88). The group then shares in the "Litany of Thanksgiving for the Generations" with group members reading the words of their representative generations (page 89).

Note to Leader:

Chapter 8, "Healing of Memories," suggests the use of a videotape that features a vignette of Frederick Buechner's working through his unresolved feelings over the suicide of his father. If you wish to pursue this option, use the following information to order the video:

Sacred Stories with Frederick Buechner, Maya Angelou, and James Carroll
Office of Video Production
Parish of Trinity Church
74 Trinity Place
New York, NY 10006
800-551-1220

7

Facing Life's Transitions

OVERVIEW

This session focuses on transitions and turning points in one's life story with special emphasis on midlife and late-life transitions that lead to significant stock taking of one's life. Three stages in transitions are explored, as well as times of meaningful coincidences.

PREPARATION

Participants have reflected on the "Taking Stock" questions and remembered turning points in their lives. Each participant will need six sheets of construction paper and a marker.

LEADING THE SESSION

Ask the group to recall any "meaningful coincidences" in the biblical stories (such as the crossing of the Red Sea or the story of Esther). Ask the group to remember any "meaningful coincidences" in their lives. When did such events occur? What happened? What did they mean?

Remind the group of the three stages that Bridges mentions in his book *Transitions*:

(1) endings, followed by
(2) a neutral zone and
(3) new beginnings.

Form participants into groups of three. One member of each triad will be the presenter who will talk about some turning point or transition in his or her life; the second is the listener who gives creative attention, speaking only to clarify what the presenter has said; and the third person is the observer who never speaks. When the presentation has ended, the observer tells the others what has been heard.

Instruct participants to use the following questions:

1. What was the transition?
2. Who were the significant persons involved?
3. What are my feelings now about that moment?
4. At which of the three stages (ending/neutral zone/new beginning) do I find myself now?
5. What are some of my former values or beliefs that no longer hold?
6. How do I find directions for this new beginning?

As time permits, the roles may shift, so each person can be presenter, listener, and observer.

Alternate Exercise

Invite the participants to turn to the stepping-stone exercise (page 101). Give each person six sheets of construction paper and a felt-tip marker. Ask members to record their stepping-stones on the construction paper. Then allow time for partners to lay out their stones, "walking" through the events in their life stories, pausing to tell about each event as they step on each stone. Encourage members to share how God was perceived and what was learned about life and faith from each event.

LOOKING AHEAD

Next week's reading assignment is chapter 8, "Healing of Memories." Encourage group members to list significant persons in their lives (see page 111), as well as people who have caused them pain (page 113). Ask them to recall times in their story when (a) they found it hard to forgive themselves, or (b) they offered forgiveness to another person who did not accept it. Urge group members to read "Scars Tell Our Story" (pages 118–19), and ask them to recall scars from their own stories. For those who enjoy the writing aspect, relay the writing assignment for chapter 8 (see Appendix 1, page 69).

CLOSING

Close by praying aloud the "Litany for Storytelling" (pages 104–105) and having participants respond with the words in bold type.

8
Healing of Memories

OVERVIEW
After recalling significant persons in one's life story, relationships of the past that need present healing are recalled. Healing of memories includes forgiving ourselves, as well as moving on when reconciliation does not happen.

PREPARATION
Group members have remembered significant persons from their stories and recalled broken relationships. Have available paper, pens or pencils. If you chose to order and view the videotape for this session, have a television and VCR ready for use.

GATHERING
Engage the group in the circle of light experience. This requires a reflective approach within the group circle. Call upon participants to remember significant persons, living or deceased, who have touched their lives. They may wish to write those names on a piece of paper or list them around the outer edge of the circle in the notebook.

In a reflective manner, ask each group member to imagine sitting in the center of a circle surrounded by those persons. Invite the participants to focus on each person in the outer circle, expressing a prayer of thanksgiving for his or her presence in life.

LEADING THE SESSION
Recall the stories of reconciliation in Genesis (Jacob and Esau; Joseph and his brothers). Consider beginning the story and con-

tinuing it around the circle. Suggest that each person begin with the words: *But before that.... or After that....* Ask the group to discuss the exercise on page 113 where they listed people who had caused them pain and then worked through the exercise to forgiveness.

Recall the biblical stories when reconciliation did not happen. Two possibilities are the conflicts between David and Absalom (2 Sam. 15:1-12; 18:1-32) and Paul and Barnabas (Acts 15:36-41). Ask the group how to move past these unresolved relationships. If the group has achieved a degree of intimacy, it might also be advisable to role-play these relationships. If possible, show the vignette of Frederick Buechner working through his unresolved feelings over the suicide of his father in the video *Sacred Stories with Frederick Buechner, Maya Angelou, and James Carroll.*

LOOKING AHEAD

Next session's reading is chapter 9, "An Ongoing Story—No Epilogue." Tell the participants to respond to the questions about their future (pages 125–26) and the questions about their death (pages 130–31). They may also wish to spend some time thinking about John David Burton's poem, "Once Again, Dime Time" (pages 129–130). For those who enjoy the writing aspect, relay the writing assignment for chapter 9 (see Appendix 1, page 69).

CLOSING

As group members read silently John C. Morgan's prayer on forgiveness (page 120), suggest that they keep in mind persons who have hurt them or whom they have hurt. Close by reading responsively "A Litany of Forgiveness" (pages 120–21).

9

An Ongoing Story—No Epilogue

OVERVIEW

Everyone has an unfinished story until dying and leaving this earth. This session helps participants reflect on the rest of their lives, their dreams, hopes, and aspirations. It also helps group members look openly at their own death, realizing we never live until we confront our mortality.

PREPARATION

Group members have already read and responded to the questions about their future life and their death. You will need one packet of twelve slips of paper for each participant for the opening exercise. Be sure to have pens or pencils available.

LEADING THE SESSION

Distribute the packets of paper and give the following instructions: On each of the small slips of paper, write one of the following:

- Three people who are very dear to you (3 slips)
- Three things you own that are very special (3 slips)
- Three activities you enjoy (3 slips)
- Three personal attributes you cherish (3 slips)

Tell the group members to arrange the twelve slips of paper in front of them so they can see all of them. Remind participants of the painful truth that with increasing health diminishment comes loss of other precious parts of our lives. Then urge the group to listen carefully as you describe the following scenarios.

You are at the doctor's office and get the diagnosis that you have incurable cancer. You have thirty seconds to decide what is less important to you; tear up three slips of paper.

You are back at home. Tear up another three slips of paper (six slips remain).

Two months later your symptoms worsen, your strength is gone, and Alive Hospice is invited to help. Tear up three more slips of paper (three slips remain).

You know your moment of death has arrived. Your family gathers, and you hand them the last three slips of paper as your ethical will. Later you die.

Ask the participants to reflect on those last three slips; what do they reveal about the values and pattern of their lives? In the next session, you will ask the participants to perceive the patterns in their life stories.

Alternate Exercise

Ask three volunteers to play the roles of the following: The Patient, who suffers from inoperable cancer; a Visitor, a Hospice volunteer who drops by for a weekly visit; and an Observer.

Ask the three participants to sit in an inner circle. The Visitor asks the following questions; the Patient responds. The Observer sits quietly as an unseen presence, offering evaluation when the interview ends. After some initial conversation, the Patient begins to talk openly about their death. The Visitor then asks the following questions:

- How do you feel about dying?
- As you visualize your final moments on earth, where would you like to be when you die?
- Whom would you like to be present?
- Whom would you like not to be present?
- Are there any prayers, scripture texts, or music you would like in your final hours?

- If possible, what would you like to say to those assembled around your bedside? your family? your friends? What would you like them to say to you?
- How do you imagine the actual moment of your death?

When the role play has ended, the Observer needs to share reflections with the Patient and Visitor. Then ask other group members to share their feelings. As time allows, you may involve other members of the group in a similar role play.

LOOKING AHEAD

In the last group session participants will reflect on the pattern they see in their life stories. Writing their life story in five sentences will help clarify the pattern. For those who enjoy the writing aspect, relay the writing assignment for chapter 10 (see Appendix 1, page 69).

CLOSING

[If possible, by candlelight]
In a reverent, quiet way, ask group members to join hands in a circle. Ask a volunteer to read aloud, "Love's Hospice" (pages 138–39). Finally, invite group members to say aloud the names of family members or friends who have died, ending the group gathering with a moment of silence.

10
Finding the Pattern

OVERVIEW

This is the closing group experience, and members may evidence some grief. For this final session, keep all sharing in the full-group context to symbolize the bonding and oneness that have developed. Through several group exercises members are led to find the patterns in their stories, as well as to become intentional about preserving their stories after the group has ended.

PREPARATION

Group members have summarized their life stories in five short sentences and should have brought them to this final session. Have available paper and pens or pencils.

LEADING THE SESSION

Ask the group members to complete this sentence fragment: *If I hadn't been born*…. After they have written their sentences, allow volunteers to say some responses aloud. Then invite the group members to close their eyes and to imagine they are standing on a high mountain, looking down on the events of their lives. Ask them to reflect on these questions:

- What patterns and themes do you see?
- Who are the people that stand out?
- How have you influenced these persons?

Allow time to share answers.

- The participant book in "Reflecting on Your Story" (page 144, question 2) suggests that persons recall one special year, a year that was a good one. By revisiting that year they can renew the joy inherent in the time both then and now. Take time to allow group members to recall their special year and the events and experiences that made it special.
- Mention that in the years ahead recollections of this group study may become special memories. Going around the circle, ask persons to relate one story that was told by another within the context of the group experience.
- Remind participants that they were to bring their life summaries (page 137). Going around the circle, ask each group member to read his or her five-sentence life summary aloud. You may want to write a bit of each summary on newsprint, which helps the members see the meaning that others have found in their life stories.
- Consider asking for summary faith statements as well. You could ask each person to begin with "I believe," followed by a statement of his or her faith.

You can ask for volunteers who may wish to share some insights about the pattern of their life story. One participant in a group, who had recently experienced separation and divorce at midlife, shared the following description of her life story, perceived through a journey of faith:

1. *Journeying from Egypt.* The single journey begins with desert time, which at first seems barren and desolate, but later becomes a moment of faith

2. *Manna in the Wilderness.* As the journey continues, cries for help are heard as friends, support groups, and other resources nourish and sustain on the journey.

3. *By the Waters of Babylon.* The darkness of despair and discouragement comes later, as being in a "Noah's ark society" means being left out and discarded.
4. *Seeing a New Way.* The world is re-fashioned, and we learn to travel the road by ourselves.
5. *The New Jerusalem.* Single life brings joy and freedom. A new life begins.

Ask the group to reflect on the five stages of the soul in Moody and Carroll's book. (In order to better understand these five stages of the soul, recall the story of Ebenezer Scrooge in Charles Dickens's *Christmas Carol*. Scrooge seems to be beyond all possible redemption. But on Christmas Eve, five stages of the soul unfold in a single night.

The Call: Jacob Marley's voice and rattling chains.

The Search and the Struggle: The Ghosts of Christmas Past, Present, and Future making Scrooge aware of his miserly past and of his mortality.

The Breakthrough: Scrooge has a spiritual transformation, dies to the old self, and is reborn.

The Return: Scrooge's life is forever changed, as his life is now spent in service and acts of kindness.

Form five small groups, and give each group one of the five stages: The Call, The Search, The Struggle, The Breakthrough, or The Return. In the smaller group each participant tries to identify some time in his or her spiritual journey when these stages occurred. Bring the whole group back together, and discuss the results.

LOOKING AHEAD

As this last group gathering draws to a close, remind the participants that their journey has only just begun. Strongly urge them to record their life stories. Offer suggestions from the Appendix of *Remembering Your Story* on writing and/or videotaping these stories. You may wish to make copies of the resources available on the Internet and hand them out to group members.

CLOSING

Allow time for members to say final words to one another and to express good-byes. As a group join in reading aloud "A Liturgy for Storytelling" (pages 155–57) and end the group meeting by passing the peace and with hugs of farewell.

Notes

1. Ann Bedford Ulanov, "Aging: On the Way to Life's End" in William Clements, ed., *Ministry with the Aging: Designs, Challenges, Foundations* (Binghamton, N.Y.: Haworth Press, 1989), 122.

2. Tristine Rainer, *Your Life As Story: Discovering the "New Autobiography" and Writing Memoir As Literature* (New York: The Putnam Publishing Group, 1997), 47 and following.

3. V. Neil Wyrick, "On the First Shelf of the Library of Heaven," (*Monday Morning*, June 1999).

4. John C. Morgan, "It's About Time: Journey toward Community," *Universalist Herald* 9 (fall 1993), 3–4.

5. Ruth E. Ray, *Beyond Nostalgia: Aging and Life Story Writing* (Charlottesville, Va.: University of Virginia Press, 2000), 133.

Written Resources for Group Leaders

Helpful Books

Doughtery, Rose Mary. *Group Spiritual Direction: Community for Discernment*. Mahwah, N.J.: Paulist Press, 1995.

Eittreim, Jean Brown. *That Reminds Me: Family Story-Starters for Passing on the Faith*. Minneapolis, Minn.: Augsburg Fortress, 1998.

Fletcher, William. *Recording Your Family History*. Berkeley, Ca.: Ten Speed Press, 1989.

Garfield, Charles, Cindy Spring, and Sedonia Cahill. *Wisdom Circles: A Guide to Self-Discovery and Community Building in Small Groups*. Collingdale, Pa.: DIANE Publishing Co., 1998.

Hopkins, Elaine, et al. *Working with Groups on Spiritual Themes: Structured Exercises on Healing*. Duluth, Minn.: Whole Person Press, 1995.

Kempthorne, Charles. *For All Time: A Complete Guide to Writing Your Family History*. Westport, Ct.: Heinemann, 1996.

Ledoux, Denis. *The Photo Scribe: A Writing Guide/How to Write the Stories behind Your Photographs*. Lisbon Falls, Maine: Soleil Press, 1999.

Leigh, David J. *Circuitous Journeys: Modern Spiritual Autobiography*. New York: Fordham University Press, 2000.

Neubauer, Joan. *From Memories to Manuscript: The Five-Step Method of Writing Your Life Story*. New York: Ancestry, Inc., 1997.

Riemer, Jack, and Nathaniel Stampfer. *So That Your Values Live On: Ethical Wills and How to Prepare Them.* Woodstock, Vt.: Jewish Lights, 1997.

Seilig, Bernard. *Writing from Within: A Guide to Creativity and Life Story Writing.* Alameda, Ca.: Hunter House, 1998.

Stone, Elizabeth. *Black Sheep and Kissing Cousins: How Our Family Stories Shape Us.* New York: Viking Penguin Books, 1989.

Examples of published life stories

Allen, Margaret P. *No Road Maps.* Hanover, Mass.: Christopher Publishing House, 1993.

Boyd, Malcolm. *Simple Grace: A Mentor's Guide to Growing Older.* Louisville, Ky.: Westminster/John Knox Press, 2001.

Ervin, Jean C. *The Youngest of Ten: An Autobiography.* Morganton, N.C.: Jean Conyers Ervin, 1997.

Legacies. Edited by Maury Leibovitz and Linda Solomon. New York: Harper-Collins, 1993.

Seaman, Paul A. *Paper Airplanes in the Himalayas: Following the Unfinished Path Home.* Notre Dame, Ind.: Cross Cultural Publications, 1997.

Periodical articles

Brown, Robert McAfee. "My Story and The Story," *Theology Today* (1975): 166–69.

Butler, Robert N. "Successful Aging and the Role of the Life Review," *The American Geriatric Society* 22 (1974): 529–35.

Capps, Donald. "Parabolic Events in Augustine's Autobiography," *Theology Today* 40 (1983): 260–74.

Hatley, B. J. "Spiritual Well-Being through Life Histories," *Journal of Religion and Aging* 1 (1985): 63–71.

Larson, Ross Henry. "Writing the Autobiography of a Person of God," *The Clergy Journal* 26 (February 2001): 34–36.

McFadden, Susan H. "Spiritual Autobiography: History and Context," Aging and Spirituality 9 (Fall 1997): 10–13.

Morgan, Richard L. "Spiritual Autobiography Groups for Third and Fourth Agers," *Journal of Religious Gerontology* 9 (2) (1995): 1–14.

Randall, R. L. "Reminiscing in the Elderly: Pastoral Care of Self Narratives," *The Journal of Pastoral Care* 40 (1986), 207–15.

Some classic autobiographies

[The following autobiographies describe the spiritual journeys of the writers and make excellent reading.]

Angelou, Maya. *I Know Why the Caged Bird Sings*. New York: Chelsea House Publishers, 1999.

The Autobiography of Benjamin Franklin. Gordonville, Va.: Saint Martin's Press, LLC, 1993.

Boyd, Malcolm. *Take Off the Masks: The Classic Spiritual Autobiography*. San Francisco: HarperSanFrancisco, 1993.

Buechner, Frederick. *The Sacred Journey: A Memoir of Early Days*. San Francisco: HarperSanFrancisco, 1991.

The Confessions of St. Augustine, trans. Carolinne White. Grand Rapids, Mich.: William B. Eerdmans Publishing Co., 2001.

Dillard, Annie. *An American Childhood*. New York: HarperTrade, 1999.

Frank, Anne. *The Diary of a Young Girl*. New York: Bantam Books, 1997.

Goodall, Jane. *Reason for Hope: A Spiritual Journey*. New York: Warner Books, Inc., 1999.

Graham, Billy. *Just As I Am: The Autobiography of Billy Graham.* Grand Rapids, Mich.: Zondervan Publishing House, 1997.

Greeley, Andrew M. *Confessions of a Parish Priest: An Autobiography.* New York: Pocket Books, 1987.

Keller, Helen. *The Story of My Life.* West Roxbury, Mass.: B & R Samizdat Express, 2000.

Mandela, Nelson. *The Long Walk to Freedom: The Autobiography of Nelson Mandela.* New York: Little, Brown, & Co., 1995.

Merton, Thomas. *The Seven Storey Mountain: An Autobiography of Faith.* San Diego, Ca.: Harcourt Trade Publishers, 1999.

Pilgrim Souls: A Collection of Spiritual Autobiographies. Edited by Amy Mandelker and Elizabeth Powers. New York: Simon and Schuster Trade, 1999. An anthology of spiritual autobiographies grouped under "Wanderers and Seekers," "Pilgrims and Missionaries," "Mystics and Visionaries," "Scholars and Philosophers."

Washington, Booker T. *Up from Slavery.* New York: Avon Books, 1976.

Doing a Church's Story

Bryant, Stephen D. "Telling the Church's Story," *Weavings* 4 (January/February 1989), 38–42, suggests ways congregations can tell their story in a storytelling workshop and turn congregational memories into a communal story.

Other Resources

Writing by Yourself
Use 100 questions in Appendix of *Remembering Your Story*
Writing tips available from:

Association of Personal Historians
www.personalhistorians.org

Story Circle Journal
P. O. Box 500127
Austin, TX 78750-0127
www.storycircle.org

Center for Autobiographic Studies
260 S. Lake Avenue, Suite 220
Pasadena, CA 91101
www.storyhelp.com

Turning Memories
www.turningmemories.com

Getting Help from Someone Else (Memoirist)

Association of Personal Historians (www.personalhistorians.com)
Offers trained and dedicated personal historians to assist people
in preserving their life stories. A membership directory is available
from the association, which will direct you to the nearest person
who can help you accomplish your goal for you and your family.

Your Life/Your Legacy Group
Contact Dr. Richard L. Morgan (E-mail: rmorgan@hci.net; phone:
828-437-4097) for workshops available in your area or ways to
schedule workshops in your area.

Share Your Life Story Workshops
Based at the Medical Humanities, University of Texas Medical
Branch, Galveston, Texas. (E-mail: MSierpina@aol.com)

Preserving Your Family Story in Brief Form
While some persons will either write or record their life stories, others may choose to preserve a briefer account as a legacy for the family. Linda Lipinski has created an album where memories may be preserved. It includes thirteen inspirational starting pages, a family tree, and pages to record marriages, births, and deaths. A photograph section holds sixteen photographs. To order:

A Legacy to Remember
RichLin Group
912 Fountain Drive
Carlsbad, NM 88220

Scripture Index for
Remembering Your Story

5 Family Relationships, Family Stories

Isaiah 51:1-2
Mark 3:33-35
Luke 15:11-32

6 Stories Connect Generations

Exodus 12:26, 27
1 Samuel 3:1
Matthew 1:18-25
Luke 1:26-56; 2:41-52
Acts 7

7 Facing Life's Transitions

Genesis 28:16
Ecclesiastes 3:1-7

8 Healing of Memories

Genesis 33:10; 45:7
1 Samuel 3
2 Samuel 17:1-4; 18:33
Luke 22:31-32, 54-62
Acts 15:39
Romans 8:28
1 Corinthians 9:6
2 Corinthians 5:20
Galatians 6:17

9 An Ongoing Story—No Epilogue

Job 5:26
Jeremiah 6:16; 32:1-15
Matthew 17
Luke 9:3; 10:38-42

10 Finding the Pattern

Psalm 23
Proverbs 31:25
Luke 24:32
Ephesians 6:13
2 Timothy 4:7

Appendix 1
Writing Assignments

Although the participant's book suggests some writing assignments, experience shows that a more structured approach to writing is beneficial. Many older adults want to write their stories. These ordinary people, none of them writers by profession or training, gather weekly to share their writings and to learn new ways of remembering and writing their life stories.

Ruth E. Ray, author of *Beyond Nostalgia: Aging and Life-story Writing*, states three norms for writing groups: (1) Members are to demonstrate an interest in one another's writings and a willingness to listen; (2) members are to support and encourage one another, creating an environment of confidentiality and trust; (3) members are not to pry, probe, or criticize the writing in any way.[5]

The following writing assignments, keyed to the participant book, have proved helpful. They are assigned at the end of the group session and brought to the next group gathering.

Writing Prompts

Chapter	*Writing Assignment*
2 *The Spiritual Lifeline*	Recall five historical events you have lived through, and write your memory of your reaction when you heard the news.
3 *The River of Life*	Visualize your life as a river, and write either a narrative or a poem.
4 *Reclaiming Childhood Stories*	Draw a floor plan of your earliest home, and write down some memories of that home.

5	*Family Relationships*	Look for photos from the past, select a photo of your family and write what is happening.
6	*Stories Connect Generations*	Select a grandparent and write about him or her.
7	*Facing Life's Transitions*	Choose a transition in your story, and write about the ending, the in-between time, and the new beginning.
8	*Healing of Memories*	Write a letter to three persons who offended or hurt you, telling them how they influenced your life.
9	*An Ongoing Story— No Epilogue*	Describe a dream for your life five years from now.
10	*Finding the Pattern*	Briefly respond to the following question: What if I had never lived? Summarize your life story in five sentences.

Appendix 2
Weekend Retreat Model

FRIDAY EVENING

7:00–8:00 After dinner the group leaders make some preliminary remarks about the goals of the retreat, using suggested material from chapter 1 of the participant book, *Remembering Your Story*. They then lead participants in a "warm-up" exercise (Leader's Guide, pages 19–20). In this way every member of the group is introduced.

8:15–9:30 Members do spiritual lifeline (participant book, pages 32–34) and then pair up to share some event or insight from the lifeline.

9:30 Closing Worship (read aloud the poem "As We Look Back in Memory," participant book, page 24) and "The Prayer of Thanksgiving for the Seasons of Life" (participant book, page 39).

SATURDAY MORNING

9:00 The River of Life guided meditation (participant book, page 46). Ask group members to share their responses to this exercise.

10:15 To get in touch with childhood faith stories, guide group members in this exercise:

- Where did you live between the ages of 6 and 12?
- Picture yourself in that home, and recall any memories as you take an imaginary walk through the rooms.
- Who was the person of warmth in your home?
- Recall a story that you identified with in that home.
- When did God become real to you in those years?

After group members write their answers, form subgroups to discuss these memories.

12:00–1:00 Lunch

1:00 Use either the Family Sculpting exercise (Leader's Guide, page 38) or Memories around the Family Meal (Leader's Guide, page 39) and possibly role-play a family meal.

2:30 Circle of Generations. Follow the exercise (Leader's Guide, pages 41–42), and allow the group to choose an issue for discussion by a panel with all five generations represented.

4:00 Free time for reflection and conversation

6:00 Dinner

7:00 Follow the Circle of Wisdom exercise (Leader's Guide, pages 42–43) after the group has chosen from the subjects listed on page 43 of the Leader's Guide.

9:00 Ask all group members to write an ethical will. (Follow the example in the participant book, page 86) and a one-paragraph summary of their faith story.

10:00 Closing Worship. Use "Litany of Thanksgiving for the Generations" (participant book, page 89).

SUNDAY

9:00 Ask participants to share ethical wills in pairs. Ask participants to turn in written life summaries and read them to the group. (Some group members prefer to read their own summaries.) You may wish to write some of the life summaries on newsprint.

10:30 Closing Worship. Allow time for members to say final words to each other and express good-byes. Lead "A Liturgy for Storytelling" in participant book (pages 155–57) and close by passing the peace.

*The publisher gratefully acknowledges permission to reprint
the following copyrighted material:*

"Across the Generations: A Dialogue." Used by permission
of Donovan Drake.

Excerpt from "It's about Time: Journey toward Community," in *Universalist
Herald* (Fall 1993). Used by permission of John C. Morgan.

"The Delta" from *The Journal Book—Fear-Anger-Love* by Carter Ossman
Muller, B.A. M.S. Copyright © 1990. Used by permission of Ossman, Inc.

"On the First Shelf of the Library of Heaven," by V. Neil Wyrick. Reprinted
by permission from *Monday Morning*, vol. 64, no. 11 (June 1999), p. 21.
Copyright © 1999 Presbyterian Church (U.S.A.), Inc.

About the Author

RICHARD L. MORGAN, an ordained Presbyterian minister, is a national leader in spiritual autobiography groups and spirituality of aging issues. He is the author of several books in the field of aging and has been leading groups across the nation for the past twenty years. He also serves as a consultant to churches wishing to form spiritual autobiography groups.